Heerman Rednick

THE HIDDEN DOOR
TO REALITY

a book
of mystical experiences

by

Herman Rednick

Open Door Publishing
Taos, New Mexico

Printed by Columbine Printing Co.
Taos, New Mexico, U.S.A.

Library of Congress Catalog Card Number 81-85124

ISBN 0-942184-00-9 hardcover
ISBN 0-942184-01-7 paperback

Open Door Publishing
is a division of Earth Journey Incorporated
a non-profit corporation
P.O. Box 485
Questa, New Mexico 87556

Other Books by Herman Rednick

The Spiritual Principle in Art
The Earth Journey

CONTENTS

Preface

Life is a mystery until you touch the reality beyond the veil. When the mind is still and the search is intense, we have the vision to see reality all around us.

Every person you meet is in a world you could know. Nature waits for our entrance, whether it is a forest or a rose. All around us is the Spirit Presence waiting for a quiet mind and an open heart. Walking through the markets and riding in the subway, we can be close to the reality. We are moving through various states of reality during the day.

H.R.

THE HIDDEN DOOR
TO REALITY

a book
of mystical experiences

SHAMBALLA

Shamballa, Sacred City of the Gods. From the dawn of time has my soul been linked to Thy Sacred City.

Shamballa, like a pure gem in the heart of the planet, glowing with prismatic radiance upon the pristine heights of the Himalayas, where men like Gods control the destiny of mankind.

Shamballa, divine focal point for the concentrated Cosmic forces which descend with great power upon Thy City, vibrating their healing light and beauty throughout the planet.

Many have been seeking Thy golden gate for centuries but find nothing but storms and fierce winds and desolate mountain peaks, for Thy Temple is guarded from the unworthy mortal. Never shall profane eyes look upon Thy ancient purity.

Beings of Light, even now do I feel the rays from the Golden City, like a divine breath exalting my body and mind and kindling the blue flame within my heart. Even as I walked through the unbearable dark Valley of Soul, O Sacred Master, I felt Thy touch and heard Thy soundless voice.

As I walk through the fields and mountains of Mother Nature I hear one voice. The fruit-laden trees speak and the silent hills at twilight whisper of the Sacred City. The whole universe breaks into a divine melody and I hear the delicate harmony of Shamballa, City of the Great White Initiates.

Thou Keeper of ancient doctrine and wisdom beyond the dream of mortal man, through You is the hope of humanity, for the future lies in Your hand.

So far away, yet so near is the White City, for my heart is linked with Thy spiritual Temple by a golden thread. And when I quiet my mind and listen to my heart, the precious inflow of Cosmic Fire sweeps over my being. This room is no more...this body is no more...for I am in complete rhythm with the Sacred City, and my being sings a melody eternal.

For many years my soul cried and searched for something, I knew not what. This body was in pain for my heart hungered for many days. Not until I felt the clear golden light of Shamballa did I understand why I longed to be in the ancient land of India.

It was because the light of the Sacred City burned within me, and the eye of a great God-like Being was upon me—One who is linked for centuries to my soul. Thus did Destiny reveal itself to me, as I turned toward the Sacred City of the Gods.

Shamballa. I utter Thy name with humility. May we be worthy to enter Thy golden gate, and may we be so purified in body, mind, and heart that Thy mantle will fall upon us.

O Great One,
Divine Cosmic Soul,
My Sacred Master,
Shamballa.

HUMILITY

In the wild deserted mountains
I met a sage sitting on a cliff.
I asked, "How can I find Truth?"
He uttered but one word.
"Humility."
And the vibrating sound of OM
filled all space
and flashed among the planets above.

I turned and asked, "Where is the Pathway?"
And he spoke one word.
"Humility."
And all the heavens and the earth
broke into musical notes
and I heard the voices of rocks,
of rivers, and of trees.

And I asked, "What shall I study,
O Sacred Master?"
And he uttered one word.
"Humility."
And I beheld a fall of flowers from the heavens
like a heavy snow at night.
The whole earth gave off a sweet fragrance
and the very air whispered,
"Humility."

SPIRITUAL GIFTS

When I give the gifts I have received from the spiritual forces, I become a clear channel for the overshadowing spirit. When I close my hand and do not give any more, the channel to the spiritual forces is closed.

If I am a radiating center for the qualities of spirit, tolerance, and universal love, the spiritual forces gather around me and I become a focal point for the forces of light, wisdom, power, and health. When I am afraid the forces encourage me. If I am weak they give me strength.

But if I discourage my brother and I do not give him understanding, then the great power I received is taken from me. For that which we receive we must share with our fellow men.

AN HOUR IN A RESTAURANT

I have an hour to spare and into a restaurant I go for a cup of coffee. I relax and am at ease in the midst of so much bustle. I think and dream, and afar I go to lands and regions that only the mind can explore. I forget the world, my cares and my desires. Detached and free, I roam through the imaginative door.

O, what a precious hour without price! And unsuspected by people, what treasures I explore! O, the precious hours are gems upon my material vesture, that keep me through the storms unharmed.

I ask for no riches or raiment of gold, but a precious hour as my abode.

UNIVERSAL MOTHERHOOD

O Divine Mother,
my heart is one with Thy soul being,
and I feel the shower of Cosmic light
when I am one with Thy spirit.
Hold my hand, O Mother Divine,
as I tread the Path
through this earth of Thine.

COMMUNION

In rhythmic breath, I sit and meditate. When my body becomes still and the brain speaks no more, I move in another rhythm and my being is in rapport with another plane. In this stillness, my Master appears to me.

THE OYSTER VENDOR

I pass an oyster vendor on the street—a plain man, an unimportant man, an uninteresting man. I stop a moment to pass over to the threshold of his being and I enter his world of thought.

I see the family he is trying to control, I see the enemies he fears, I see the things he loves and the people he hates. And back of these I see his longing heart's desire, the light that keeps him going. Through the simple oyster man I enter a fascinating world.

AUM

I stood upon a mountain and I saw before me a circle of Masters. They invited me to meditate with them. I took my place in the circle and we began to chant the sacred Word, AUM. My attempt was like the "peek" of a bird in the face of a great thunderstorm. AUM vibrated through the mountains with tremendous power.

My body seemed to burst, and my being filled the universe. I beheld the stars and heard them sing AUM, and I saw the White Brothers descend upon the beam of AUM.

Then the atoms of my body were shot back into place, and I returned to a clay temple that throbbed with the song of the universe. AUM became my breath, my mind, and my life.

THE DARK NIGHT OF SOUL

The wet darkness of hopeless despair stretches before me in an endless night. Could God have this hell created, such painful monotony and lifeless existence torturing me in a place like this? But my words were only drowned by the black walls of futility and negation. I know there is a brighter land beyond, if I could only tear this veil before me.

But I was helpless in this region damned, and compelled to march through this painful valley until purified of my earthly dross. A stranger I beheld walking, clothed in black from head to foot, and he spoke unto me, saying, "This region is your own creation. You must travel through this Dark Valley until prepared for a higher plane."

CHIEF RISING SUN

When I gazed upon your face, I did not look upon a stranger, for I beheld a brother of the Cosmic Spirit, a soul whose heart was the sun.

Chief Rising Sun, you are mellowed by the sun and moon and the planets, and in your eyes I see the light of another universe. The sea and wind, the earth and sky sing a melody for a soul who has weathered every storm and arrived in the harbor of the Great Spirit. Your body has become the Temple, radiant with healing for the world.

I can hear Mother Earth say, "I am proud of you, my son. You are the flower of this planet. For a million million years I labored and you are the product of my toil, the jewel of my heart."

MEDITATION

Invocation is the first step toward realizing the necessity of a close relation with the spiritual forces. It is the universal approach toward God, from the chanting of the Africans in the jungle, the sun worshippers at dawn, to the Great Invocation of the Masters upon the Himalayas Who vibrate the whole planet with Their power. Our call is heard according to our sincere intensity and understanding. We can bring the very Gods among men.

ADVICE TO A FRIEND

I see before me a pit of humans with hysterical fixed stare, chasing phantoms of gluttony and sensuality. I see some striving to turn from this electrical whirlpool of illusion, struggling to free themselves from this hypnotic lie of materialism. But they have waited too long. They are blind and cannot see the way.

I say unto you standing at the entrance, arise while there is light within you and taste of that pure joy of reality that is above and beyond decaying mortality. When will you learn your lesson? Must you burn to be cleansed of your materiality?

ART OPENS THE DOOR

I am painting again. Fourteen beautiful color notes upon a white palette, and a clean canvas upon the easel. What infinite possibilities it has.

I thank God as I approach this canvas, and as I lift my brush my being reaches out into space. My heart bursts into light and the spirit comes upon me like some summer breeze.

I am transported to a world of spirit and power, and before my gaze new worlds are formed. I place my brush upon the palette and with the fourteen color notes, a new art being is born upon this plane.

I ENTERED A RIVER DOMAIN

I sat beside the river and she spoke unto me, saying, "Come to my domain." I entered and became a river and flowed down the narrow banks.

I love to feel the mud and rocks on my river bed. The feeling of fish and the creatures within my body gives me hope for another day, for unto them I give life. I flow through the meadows and disappear into the sea.

OUR HOME

This home of God and mind is the sacred focal point for Thy light, O Divine Mother. I behold a great flash of Cosmic power burst in this sacred abode and vibrate throughout the planet. I dare not think or act not according to Thy law, for then I see the painful dimming of this great light, and it breaks my heart. For what is a home without Thee, O Divine Mother?

FORSAKEN

Blackness rolls before me
and the spinning earth disappears
beneath my feet,
and I hang like some forlorn ghost
in a great void.

O Mother Spirit,
touch my brow with Thy cool hand.
Tell me not that all have forsaken me so.

The dread of night upon me hangs.
I cry out again
but all is silent.
How long must I endure this agony,
O Universal Mother of mine?

VALHALLA

I walked through pools of blood, insane with the desire for battle, crazed by the waves of hatred that were sweeping the nation. I met my end in a lonely outpost and dropped like a discarded garment on an unknown and unmarked grave.

I awoke with the blast of the trumpet, and found myself ascending the stairway of a red stone building with my rifle still in my hand. I entered a great blue hall where all the dead had gathered together to learn the lesson of universal brotherhood and to worship the same Cosmic Mother.

ETERNAL FRIENDSHIP

We are bound by the eternal thread of friendship. Our souls did meet and merge in a symphony of the other worlds. As we rise in consciousness from state to state, from world to world, a new vision will open upon us while we walk along the Path in the Cosmos—a new vision of true friendship where soul with soul flows and blends in celestial song.

And we can look back, lives without number, and see the golden thread of friendship link us together, and we see the Hand of Destiny move us and cross our paths at the destined moment. Ancient friends meet in a new and strange world to reawaken the ancient tie.

I look into the future to new worlds. What form will you wear when you cross my path again? What will I wear when I cross your path? Ah, the mystery of life in the eternal tie of friendship.

THE EAGLE

I saw an eagle upon a cliff. My spirit moved across space and entered the eagle, and I became an eagle, king of this region before me.

Is there any bird that shall defy me? I sail through the air and circle over the broad valley. I swoop down in a spiral with my eye on my prey. As I approach a stream, I dive, and plunge into the water. I rise with several sweeps of my strong wings and fly over the field and disappear into the mountain beyond.

THE THING LIVED

I watched my mother wash a tub,
a tin wash tub.
With a palm full of water
and with a steady stroke,
She washed the side of the tub.
With a steady stroke of love for the thing,
with a steady stroke of love for the form,
with a steady stroke of love for the material.

With a magnetic stroke of love
it became alive
with sympathy and character.
With a magnetic stroke of love
it was transformed, and lived,
part of my mother's life and expression.

MAYAN CEREMONY

I heard the rhythmic beat of a large drum, and I heard the voice of the high priest calling unto the Gods, to the rhythm of the beating drum, an invocation to the Gods, as the priest offered his sacrifice upon the burning altar.

The priest intoned his invocation in rhythm with the spirit forces. The drum called upon the spirit forces, their wills demanded the spirit forces, the sacrifice called the spirit forces.

The calling of the name of the spirit forces compelled them to descend before the priest. And the sacrifice on the altar gave the spirit forces the means to materialize and take form before them.

I POUR MY SOUL UPON THE EARTH

I blew a trumpet and it blazed throughout all
space. I saw a white light appear upon a mountaintop. From this light a being stepped forth.
It was my own soul there in that fire divine,
yet here upon earth did my shell remain. He
stretched forth his hands and all space vibrated
with musical notes, and a heavy dew fell upon
the earth.

The multitude gave up their gratitude for a
great blessing, and then the being entered the
flame and disappeared. My life went with him,
and my shell crumbled into dust.

BEFORE THE TEMPLE GATE

Toward the Temple gate I moved in a boat fashioned out of will and love to the wisdom of the Temple within.

POLAR BEAR

What great power does your head contain, white, large polar bear? I perceive the powers that made you, and I hear a great rumbling under the earth, of forces. I see it concentrate and form and your head emerge. I look into the fire of those eyes and I hear a great flash of light burst through the heavens and light the fire in your eyes. I watch the rhythm of your walk and I see the flowing line of mountains and running streams. You are the full expression of Nature, white, large polar bear.

TRANSPORTED BY A FRIEND

When I left you, my being broke into a light. I walked upon an astral plane that seemed like a gigantic harp swept by a wind, and sounded like the rush of many waters. And I heard a delicate music that filled me with pure joy. My being sang with the tone of the spheres, because my friend walked in rhythm with me.

ON A MOUNTAIN

On a great mountaintop I climbed
and I beheld a vista serene.
And if my mind
the Mount of Soul would climb
and attain that serenity
where the mountain and sky unite,
so would I merge with reality.

DEATH AND IMMORTALITY

The fear of death hangs like a menacing cloud over civilization. But when we overcome this fear and realize that life is an unbroken line of development, at once a new freedom comes upon us. And we no longer feel as if some shadow were lingering nearby, for we know that we do not dwell in time, but that we stand at the Threshold of Eternity. When one is seeking for the Light, some imaginary or astral experience will come to us and reveal that death is but a shadow, and in reality is the gateway to greater knowledge and unfoldment. Let us go into the world of imagination and watch someone pass the threshold.

The time has come to depart from this world of flesh and suffering. Why do my friends mourn for me? I would speak to them, but my tongue does not move and my thoughts go unspoken. I do not feel my body any longer. It is becoming very dark, and suddenly I see a burst of orange light around my head. Then blackness rolls upon me again.

When I see light again, I find myself hovering over my body, free and light. And a great sense of relief came over me. I spoke again to those beside my body, and said, "Please do not mourn for me." But they did not hear me.

31

I hear some music like a harp. I burn, and I behold a being at a doorway who bids me enter a dazzling land of liquid light.

HIDDEN EGYPT

I meditate upon Egypt and its wisdom, aged like the cool sands beneath the Nile and as firm as the rocks beneath the Great Pyramid— a great symbol of wisdom through the ages, from some great epoch now sunk beneath the Pacific. I breathe deep as I utter the word, "Egypt."

This room becomes dim, and cool winds sweep across my face. And I see the Pyramid rise before me, and its gigantic rock walls seem like eternal sentinels. I move across the hot golden sand and push through the thick walls as one moves through a heavy fog—and find myself in the silence of a dim, hidden corridor. I walk along and move through the silent vaults of heavy darkness which seems to creep and hang like a cloak upon me.

I seem to drop down. And I find myself in a secret crypt of black marble, sealed for ages from time and the profane look of man. I stand in awe before the sacred chamber of mystery and wisdom of the kings.

SPIRITUAL LOVE

Were the worlds to spin and break before my gaze and the waters cover the face of the globe, I would not fear, because I love a friend who understood. If blackness descended upon the earth I would not care. I could be radiant and happy because a friend I love can merge with me.

I could walk through roaring flames and be burnt to ash if thy subtle presence walks with me. No dark power or demon unseen could stay me from my appointed task when thy love dwells with me. The quake and storm, the flux and change are naught when your love dwells in me.

DISILLUSIONED

O stupid one! Out of material nothings thou hast created a mountain. Out of illusion thou hast created a God. Lost in the mirage of false beliefs, wandering like a lost ship on a starless sea.

I shall rend this creation from heaven to earth, and I will crush this world with my hands! I shall cast my vision into the eternal realm and my mind shall harbor an eternal note which will bridge me across the gulf of illusion into my own native land.

INSPIRATION

In the stillness of the night I hear the voice of an invisible guide. A vision appears before me which illuminates my heart with a strange fire. Into the depths of thought I wander. To the heights I ride on a beam of love.

I yearn to express my revelation. I create a symbol, and it bears an impress of the infinite.

A RARE UNION

When two souls can love each other spiritually and commune from the depths of their being, what greater manifestation of Thy Plan and Purpose is there upon this earth, O Master?

BUT NATURE WAS SILENT

For a delicate form
I sought eagerly among the woods.
Watching, watching for your spiritual form,
for an exalted smile and a head of gold.
But the trees were silent
and the sky did not speak,
and my jewel did not appear.

But I looked on,
hoping for a radiant countenance
to break the silent wood.

THE CATHEDRAL

I enter through an arch of angels into the cool silence of a cathedral. Dark mystic vaults, like huge caverns, fill me with awe. The pillars rise in majestic unison and seem to break into a shower of jewels in the light of the stained glass above, as if to pour a holy blessing upon the thirsty souls below. The holy pain of a million souls gave birth to this divine structure.

THE GOLDEN CITY

Beyond the reach of man and the touch of elemental forces, glows a City like a jewel in the heart of the planet.

GUARDIAN OF THE THRESHOLD

In an unknown astral region, the Great Guardian of the Threshold arose from the depths of the earth with thundering light and power. He challenged my entrance to this forbidden region of another world.

I stood still and did not fear, for the light was aglow within my heart. My will was strong and my being pure, so unafraid I stood. Within me was the God of Power—that I affirmed—and I knew that no other force could harm a fortified soul.

The Guardian said, "You are afraid to cross my path."

I answered, "The God within does not fear."

He said, "Your body is unclean and not ready."

I replied, "The God within is pure."

He said, "You do not have the will."

Then I almost screamed back, "God within me is the power and the will and I am not afraid!"

Then the Great Guardian rolled into a cloud and disappeared.

MY ETERNAL COUNTERPART

For a thousand lives I have searched for my counterpart throughout the centuries. My soul hungered for a being who embodies the counterpart of my soul.

In some dream world I found myself upon the Sun, and my being blazed forth with Cosmic light and power. As I looked across the cool stellar spaces, I beheld my divine counterpart upon the Moon. There was a flash of fire between us. Her being was fashioned out of Cosmic substance, which showered upon space sparks of divine love.

The Sun and Moon moved swiftly to Their destined meeting, and when the two great planets merged, there was a flash of light among the stars. And when I became one with my counterpart, a melody resounded throughout the universe to that timeless unbeginning where the worlds have their birth.

NEW MOON MEDITATION

I sit on a hill in the calm of the night. The new moon is casting its magnetic power upon the earth and calling me to meditation.

So still becomes the body as I sit in rapt contemplation upon the spiritual truth of man, and how sweet is the fire that burns within my heart.

Peace descends in great waves upon my body and mind. The Spirit forms a ring of light around me as the invisible forces gather in great power round about me. Within this circle of light, Cosmic Beings descend before me upon a field that has been prepared by the invisible forces. And this sacred ground is protected by a circle of light. Within this circle of high vibration, the great Masters of the Cosmos descend and commune with me.

SON

When I heard you say, "Son," it was like a universal song, as if some gigantic being from the stars above came down and struck this earth with a rod, and the mellow sound thereof was, "Son, Son, Son."

It went out into the stellar spaces and vibrated throughout the worlds. How beautiful is the sound of the word, "Son, Son, Son."

A KINDRED SOUL

I touched your inner being when I set my gaze upon your face, O sensitive soul. I know you well, for no time nor fashion nor age can change the kindred tongue we speak. I see beneath your raiment the flame of soul's desire, reaching out for some sympathetic being. No sharp word or crack of whip will teach thee or show you the way, but the kind words of some loved one will pour like some divine lotion upon your being.

A TEMPLE ACROSS THE SEA

I thirst for knowledge and search among books. I found no key to the realm I sought and did not know where to go.

I cried out into space to the Masters of Wisdom, to the Lord of the Universe. My cry did not go unheard, nor was my intense thirst for knowledge unseen.

In a temple far across the sea, on a mountain far above the valley of men, the Masters I searched for were searching for me. They heard my cry and They answered my need. They came to me in spirit and instructed me in many things.

And They always continued to watch me as I go my way through the world that leads to the temple far across the sea. No sea or fire or height or depth shall keep me from the Masters in a temple waiting for me.

MAN AND THE ROSE

In the palm of my hand, this delicate flower I held. With my fingers I separated the inner petals. It seemed to shrink from my claw of flesh, for it said in a very quiet voice, "I'm spirit. You see nothing but the shadow of my heart."

Abashed, I laid the flower down, self-conscious of my heavy body of flesh and bones. I closed my eyes and thought, and tried to purify my soul. In rapt silence I sat.

I open my eyes and I see a holy flower of spiritual light. I extend my large clumsy hand to touch this sacred thing, but the light vanished and left me the shadow of the thing.

THE PLIGHT OF AN ARTIST

My palette has gathered dust
and my paint is dry and hard.
While the sun swings over the heavens
and sets in beauty
my soul is cold and my canvas bare.

Will my stagnant cell
receive a flash of light
from the circle and order beyond,
so that my palette may flow with color
and my canvas an eternal idea bear?

THE ENCHANTED RAVINE

I stepped out of the sunlight into a cool shadow of a ravine. The tender ferns greeted me, so that I felt at home beside the brook. A very old tree towered overhead. His hoary form seemed like a wise guardian of this retreat. I sat on a mossy rock and watched the brook as it danced through the shadows.

It was an interesting place, yet a strangeness filled the air. It looked like the home of gnomes and sylphs. I expected a form to come out from the old tree. If it weren't for the tender ferns that spoke, I would not linger in such a place. One can never tell. If vision came upon me, I might behold a host of goblins and dwarfs.

ETHERIC RECORD OF ANCIENT EGYPT

Out of the tombs of Egypt, a small clay figure I held before me. I took it in hand, and with rhythmic breath I went into the breathless silence of my inner being.

I moved back across the centuries into that mystic land of Egypt, and I beheld a beautiful palace interior, the wrappings of mummies; and dazzling white cities appeared before me.

I rode upon the vibration of this clay figure into the etheric heart of Mother Nature, which contains the records of all things, all peoples from the beginning of time.

MOTHER

I sought for a wondrous soul far and wide,
when near at hand a sacred light
I had overlooked,
who with bleeding step and in noble silence
sacrificed herself on the altar
of pure love,
so that we may grow like strong oaks
and stand the storms of experience.

Thy subtle love and golden soul
thy children do not understand,
for selfish pursuits have blinded their eyes
from the priceless pearl
that is so near at hand.

SENSIBILITY

Did you ever feel a plant, a flower, feel as though it were in your heart and not on the table, as if your soul were feeling its form and weight and growth?

AMONG THE HILLS

I go out among the hills on a grey and quiet day. Those distant hills have a beautiful blue note, a color I love to see. It seems to strike a chord within my being.

My spirit goes out to the hills and roams over the land. Across the field my spirit races, over the gentle rise and fall of the land. I dart up the sharp rise of the mountain and down through the rhythmic slopes. I blend with the delicate symphony of translucent greys, blacks, and browns.

My spirit returns to its clay dwelling refreshed. My eyes a material world beheld, but my being a world of spirit explored.

A BODY OF IMMORTAL LIGHT

In the far-flung waste places of Tibet
we lived on books and prayers
for twenty years or more,
seeking the truth we came here for.
My reward came when my body grew old
and in its place a body of immortal light
did I behold.

I am free from the doctrine
and the material methods I employed,
and now I roam the universe
as a free being, unalloyed.

This old body of mine I am ready to discard,
for I know it is only a garment of flesh
for this earth plane upon which I roamed.
I behold eternal vistas beyond,
far from material dreams,
and only with a body of immortal light
can I the other world explore.

So, material garment of flesh,
you served me well.
but I am glad to leave you.
To the dust return.

O PLANET EARTH

O Earth, planet of man, spinning in a sea of stars with worlds so vast and mysterious. O Mother Destiny, what have You in store for this troublesome planet? What place has man in Your scheme? You have made him equal with the Gods and You have made man a little lower than the worm.

The glory that robed the planet is no more. The mysteries are asleep and the Temple is barren.

What hope have You for man, Divine Mother? And what hope is there for the nations, this ball of earth, shooting through a wilderness of worlds, a globe spinning in the vastness of space into the unknown future of creation.

A SUDDEN TRANSFORMATION

Suppose, all of a sudden, something happened here—my body is destroyed, too suddenly for me to realize that I have crossed the threshold.

I find myself in the astral world in a class, an exact duplicate of this one. I don't know that I passed over until some light movements of the body and the instantaneous transportation from one place to another give me the idea that I am living in another region. I am not sure of my condition until some stranger walks into the class and tells me what has really happened.

Instantly, the first thing I did was look around for my body. But I was told of the futility of my search.

Before I go on my journey, I see the panorama of my whole life pass before me, from the time of birth up to the present. My loves and hates, joys and sorrows, triumphs and failures pass before me. That which seemed important on earth, I see as a trifle, and that which seemed of no importance, I see as an important factor in life.

I say, "If only I could descend into the world again, if I could take on the cloak of flesh once more, I would move through life a different being and try to show humanity the precious things I see."

As a last wish, the forces give me a temporary body, and I make my descent upon the earth. I look upon the face of humanity with different eyes. Why do they look so worried, and so fearful, straining their minds and bodies after so many unnecessary things and vain ambitions? I reach out my hand to give them my knowledge. All but a few turn from me. My new concept of life has separated me from the world. I am alone among a million souls.

I turn my gaze back to that astral region where I met people who understood each other, and where various types of humanity are attracted according to their kindred natures and states of evolution.

In a moment I disappeared from the world and was back in the other region. My cloak of flesh was dissolved, and I went on my journey through the higher worlds.

NATURAL RHYTHM

Have you felt the rhythm of the hills?
Do trees convey silent messages to you?
Will words ever speak my vision?
Can Art tell my story?
Divine Wisdom, answer me.

BACK ACROSS THE CENTURIES

As we travel back through the centuries, we will find that the nations that have produced great and lasting Art are the nations that have delved deeply into the inner chambers of their beings and have contacted the great universal Source of wisdom and power through their systems of metaphysics and occult philosophy.

A STRUGGLE WITH THE
MATERIAL FORCES

When I took my first steps on the White Path, the dark forces rushed against me and formed a black wall around me. Here I sat while the thin thread of light descended upon me from my Master. I was here until I gathered enough strength of will and understanding to rise out of the pit.

THE CALL

The call of my Master to carry the Truth to the multitude struck an unquenchable fire within my being. I am conscious of my Master's presence, and I care not about the suffering that I bear nor the criticism hurled at me, when I know that some beings on this earth seek the food that I have to give. The voice of my Masters is like the clean breath from the sea, which heals my being with waves of Cosmic love.

FRIENDS WITH A TREE

I have made friends with a tree.
We are beginning to understand each other.
We have something in common.
I feel its essence.
It conveys silent messages to me.
We love each other.

MY FRIEND IS SICK

I walked into the sickroom of a friend who had called for me. She looked up at me with a painful expression and gasped, "Please help me!"

My heart pained and my whole body and mind and soul cried out to the Great Forces of the etheric spaces. And a warm glow appeared within my heart, and a peace and quiet descended upon the room like the breathless stillness of dawn. My call was answered.

And I turned to look at my friend, and she was fast asleep. The shade of serenity settled upon her brow and peace flowed upon her form like the moonlight upon a river, as if the monster of the shadows had let her go when a divine light beamed from above.

FOURTH DIMENSION

With the power of concentration I penetrated beyond into the realm of the fourth dimension. Persistent effort built up the vibration that liberated me from the body.

With a strong will I sailed out of the body into the infinite sea of spirit and beauty. It was my will that took me to my desired places. It was the love within the heart that protected me from undesirable forces. It was the quality of courage that pushed open the door to the higher world.

How well I realize that without these qualities, it would be dangerous to open the door to the other world. Now I understand why the Masters have stressed the importance of such qualities.

THE WHITE INITIATE OF EGYPT

Free from the mortal coil I roam the worlds.
The universe is my home. My heart beats with
the Cosmic rhythms of the sun, the stars, and
the planets across the heavens.

PURE ART

He who is selected and has selected the life of an artist divine, let him prepare for his work in thought purified, with mind developed supreme. And his form, that is technique, and his mind, that is spirit, progress side by side. For form alone is not Art, and spirit alone without form is Art unmanifested.

And he will advance in humility, love, and wisdom. For without love, there can be no Art, for love is the foundation, the breath, length, and depth, and structure of Art. Without the quality of love, the form is vacant nothingness.

A YOUTH COMES TO ME

A youth comes to me for help. He is tense and eager for knowledge, and his eyes are like balls of fire. His whole being cries out and says, "Feed thou my soul, O teacher, feed thou my soul!"

I enter his soul region upon the bridge of his sincere intensity, and I water the ground with divine light.

DESTINY

O Destiny, Divine Mother, Thy billion spirit children cover the earth, and Thy rays of light and power are carried to their appointed places to evolve the light and destroy the dark.

SILENT COMMUNE

After my coffee in a restaurant, I gaze upon the faces about me. There were strange faces, curious faces, cold faces, and kind faces.

I see one face that strikes a chord within my being. My thought goes out to that person. It surrounds and investigates that being. A brief moment, and there is a silent communion of souls. We both recognize the sign.

We go on our ways, never to meet again, but I carry a recharged soul that drank deeply from a silent commune.

UNIVERSAL SOUL

O Universal Love, Thy power has sustained every heart, and every creature upon the earth is Thy sacred Being. My friends across the sea and in the far corners of the globe are nourished at Thy breast, and drink at the fount that gave me my being. I cry with joy at the unity of all men and women and beasts and creeping things, for they all live on Thy universal breath.

In darkness do all people subdivide and in small circles withdraw, and with false disguises of various names think they are apart and above.

O Universal Mother-Father-God, Thy infinite compassion endures the blindness of men. When they awaken from that world illusion, they will find one great Power, one Truth, and one Substance permeating all beings, all creatures, and all things.

WORLD OF GNOMES

In order to reach that Ivory Temple of learning, I had to ride through the Dark Valley, the region of the elementals.

As I descended into the gnome world, it became very cold and dreary. I heard a buzzing sound, like an old sawmill, fill the place. And I beheld the queen of gnomes with scepter of power in hand, come toward my roadway. I was seized with fear, but instantly turned toward the Great White Hosts for help. A cloud formed above and enveloped me with an invisibility until the queen was far beyond the hill. I went on my way, watching the small, dwarf-like creatures. They did not utter the buzzing sound I heard, but the air itself seemed to give it forth.

As I ascend out of this gruesome plane, the air became warmer and freer. When I reached the top of the cliff, I was in my own plane of activity. There was a scent of flowers in the air and a golden glow was upon the whole landscape. On the blue distant hill, I beheld my destination, the Temple of Knowledge, glowing in its white pristine purity.

ATTRACTION

I thought
and it appeared.

I desired
and it came unto me.

I doubted
and it disappeared.

A CUP

A white cup.
A coffee cup.
I look on
and see a cup
of significant form
and perfect color.
It reveals great beauty.

THE SPOKEN WORD

A spoken word carries the tone of your being in whatever state you may be in. You can ride in upon the vibration of a word and can enter the inner recesses of a man's being.

A word has the power to create or to destroy if the person who speaks it is sufficiently illuminated. If an Initiate gives a command, His words go forth like a shot, a highly concentrated nucleus of energy and power that spins and evolves out of the elements of the universe the form given by its creator.

This is especially so on the higher planes of vibration, where a thought of fear will go from you like a flash of lightning, and a thought of love will create a light. The word of an Adept would vibrate throughout the planet like thunder and would generate enough power to create a new world.

It is written, "It was spoken and it was done." It is true among the Universal Forces and is true with a lesser meaning among men.

CREATIVE FORCES

He has become master of himself. Therefore he has learned to master the forces of the universe. His body is no longer subject to decay because he lifted his mind to a Cosmic vibration, which in turn transmuted the cells of the body.

With will he put the body in a deep sleep and he walked out of the body in his spirit. In spirit he rose up in space on the magnetic forces and stood on a planet far from the earth.

From this planet he rose up in space and stood in the blackness of the vast unknown. There he was sustained by a spiritual force which formed like a hand beneath his feet. His being radiated with light against the deep background. Everything was a rich, velvety blackness, with the stars as great lamps suspended in air.

The Master stretched forth His hand and the black light rolled through His hands, full of power. The Master called out into space the sacred Word and a tone went forth in space. A great thundering noise rushed through space and passed like a mighty wind through the Cosmos. And out of this wind great bolts of light went ripping through the darkness.

The Master held out His hands and called to the forces. They descended through His hand and passed on into space, carrying out the idea the Master had impressed on them with His will.

THE MOB SPIRIT

The hate and anger of the mob attracted the
beasts of the lower worlds. These elemental
spirits feed on the hate and lust of human
beings. The spirits become inflated to tremendous size, holding the humans in their hypnotic trap and carrying them to doom and destruction.

UNSEEN POWER

I will stretch forth my arm over land and sea
and I shall build a wall with invisible hands
and with invisible bricks construct my defense.
And I shall stay the enemy,
even the invisible enemy I will stay.

VOICES OF NATURE

Nature beckoned me enter the solitary wood.
I retired into the wilderness.
A hermit's paradise.
Nature spoke through color forms.

I love to hear the running brook sing.
And the sun smiled upon the forest.
The mountain watches me all day.
Peace reigns at twilight.
The forest knows a kindred spirit.

A thousand forms danced beside the brook.
Several trees lingered while the whole forest
        was asleep.
I beheld before me an enchanted forest.

When I spoke aloud the trees remained silent.
Strange forms sleep in the rocks.
The birches shimmer in autumn gold.
The trees vibrated in prismatic glory.
What did the seven birches say?

A hill exalts all things.

I looked beyond the green and purple forms.
The sunset is full of magic.
A mist transformed the mountain.
I walked the road at twilight.

The earth, sky and mountains rejoice.
An old oak greeted me.
The old guardian of my retreat.
This must be some other world.
Forest Spirit, you are the gate to another world.

I draw my power from the sun.
The trees face east.
The day was spun from gold and precious gems.

The birch grove.
A host of spirit forms greeted me in the wood.
Here I lived and found the key to Nature.

With the rain came memories.
The earth, sky, and my home breathed in
    rhythm.

Like a ruby glowed the maple in the forest
    green.
The sleeping forest left brown and grey upon
    her forms.
At sunset the heavens broke into a Cosmic
    symphony.
Flames of red and gold enveloped the pines.
Did the colors dance before the oak?

I entered a mystic grove.
The trees spoke to me without voice.
The healing shadows of fragrant pine.

The hills struck a note through the valley.
Wind and forest merge with song.
Peace vibrated in the woods.
You always greeted me, O friendly birch.
In the cool shadows, I dreamed of another
      world.
Ah, mystery, stillness.

AMONG THE STARS

Swiftly through space, like a flash on the wings of thought, I ride through the universe. With lightning speed I pass the stars. Many days I journey through the Milky Way until my heart is heavy and my head is low, for nowhere is Truth to be found.

There is a flash of light and the current breaks. All is silent when I awaken in my abode. And I hear a voice say, "Truth is within."

MY MASTER

Silence falls like a soft cloak upon me. Universal currents flow upon my being like moonbeams upon a river. My heart bursts into a warm light and my being sounds off the healing rays of Cosmic power. I breathe enraptured the presence of God as the seven stars within my soul sing to the worlds in the stellar spaces above.

In this still stillness, Thy Sacred Presence I feel, O my Sacred Master. I feel the charge of Your power fill this room and break like a shower of stars. This room becomes the antechamber of another world. With scepter in hand, I rise to the world above.

SPIRIT BODY

I have a spirit body of light and love. I travel
in the transparent realm of universal mind.
Free and fearless, among the planes of thought
I roam.

IN THE SUBWAY TRAIN

In a row of people before me, I see a face that stops my wandering gaze. You are known to me, yet I never met you.

In spirit I walk across the car and enter your mental world, and there I hold conversation with you like an old friend. I see you are in need, so I advise and encourage you and give you strength. You are aware of something happening to your being, something strange and wonderful.

I never saw you before and shall never see you again. What was our instantaneous contact based on? Is there an ancient bond of soul between us?

NEGRO SPIRITUAL

I hear the wail of the race soul ring throughout
the mountains. I hear the hope of a people in
the song of a Negro spiritual.

SACRIFICES UNTO A WAR GOD

The great war monster accepts only the dead victims as a sacrifice. The deep river of blood flows as a testimony to the curse upon civilization. Heaven and earth quake with the prayer of wailing widows for peace on earth and good will toward men.

TO JEAN

Give me the magic rod,
O Lord of Destiny,
so I may collect a cup of light
that is flowing from my soul,
and make a golden key for the gate
to the worlds I know.

That is the greatest offering I have to give you,
my spiritual friend. It would be an eternal
treasure, much greater than any material thing
I know. My love for you will give me the
power to materialize my heart's desire.

COSMIC CONSCIOUSNESS

Man enters Cosmic Consciousness when personality is subdued and the body is controlled, when the mind is ripe with learning and the heart is open with love, when we take all humanity as our family and we do not recognize any barriers between races, creeds, or stations, when we look for reality beyond the surface of things seen or heard and beyond the border of the hypnotic stream of mortality, when we dedicate our lives to the spiritual ideas instead of the material goal of the world, and when we are persistent in our search for truth and our lives are consistent with our ideals. Then the treasures of the Gods are given to men, and this gift is recognized as the state of Cosmic Consciousness.

COSMIC SPIRIT OF ART

I move throughout all space and time and time-less eternity. I am the breath of the Egyptian culture and mysteries. I am the flower of the Greek art and philosophy. I have inspired the great souls throughout the ages, because I am the beginning and the end. Through the worlds visible and invisible I move. And I come to you through the manifestation of this symbol, this work of art.

MARION

Upon life's threshold, a child fair and pure.
Your destiny God knows. And with faith in
the still small voice you will ride upon the
angel's robe to the City of Gold and rivers of
living light. So listen, dear child, to the voice
always at your side.

THE INNER TEMPLE

When I gained sufficient understanding, I was lifted above the material plane of vibration, and I found myself in a Temple of spirit, made without hands, in the realm of a higher world. No pride or self existed there, or sense of competition, but an intense feeling of brotherhood, which united every person present with a sense of love and reverence toward each other, and which I have never beheld in another world.

In this state of unity and love, what great wisdom came into our circle! What new realms of understanding were opened because we were perfectly attuned in love and reverence toward each other. Each shared the other's thoughts without saying a word. Understanding flowed from heart to heart in a rhythm that can only be attained in spirit.

The truths taught here are too sacred for any mortal lips to utter. The truths are embedded deep in the heart of every one present like so many precious jewels.

And when we returned to our mortal bodies of flesh, what a divine radiance we brought back—not to keep, but to radiate for the good of our fellow men.

INTERNATIONAL ME

International me—in every country I dwell, and to no nation do I belong. Yet all people are my people, and every nation is my nation.

HATE SWEEPS A NATION

The terrific forces of hate engulf the nation in
a black whirlpool of destruction, feeding the
beasts of the lower worlds.

THE HEART OF THE WORLD

My being is one with the universal Heart. My heartbeat throbs in the Heart of the world and vibrates through the seven planes and strikes a tone among the planets above.

I give my body to be crucified like Thine, O Master, so that the serpent power may rise and burst in Cosmic Fire within this clay temple, so that my rays may attract even the little children, who bring heaven upon this material plane.

May Thy Symbol burn with everlasting Fire within my heart, O Master, so that I may be worthy of Thy sacrifice, and to follow within Thy footsteps.

MATERIAL MAN

I have a body of clay and stone.
A mighty river runs through me.
The quake of yonder mountain
beats and vibrates within me.
It roars in the valley,
it rumbles through the mountains.
Like an oak I lift my arms
to the sky.
Earth and mountains are in me
and I in them.

I tread the solid roadway
and merge with yonder mountain.

WORLD OF LIGHT AND DARKNESS

I enter the door of harmony. Angels soar up and down my being and fill me with power. I pour forth to all as it descends upon my being.

I return to a lower world and seem to walk through a dark valley. I am so lonely as I walk through this valley. No one knows me, nor can anyone reach me. Is this the price I pay for the rare privilege of having forces of light pour through my being?

I AM UNIVERSAL

No race or nation or group clings to my being, for I have withdrawn from the small circles upon the earth into the clear strata of universal consciousness, through the Cosmic Fire rising within my being.

I stand on top of the planet embracing all nations and all people. I look out into the vast stellar spaces and behold the Cosmic current passing through the planets, descending upon this earth of ours, and permeating all Nature and every human being—one Cosmic breath, breathing through all humanity.

I turn toward a brilliant planet and stretch forth my arms, and I feel a delicate magnetic wave pass over me. And I behold before me a being from that starry orb who, with radiant smile, says, "We are all sustained by the same Cosmic Mother."

WHITE BROTHERHOOD

I hear a clash of cymbals and a rolling of thunder through space. And there appeared the mighty God in the heavens Whose face of golden light illuminated the universe. The great serpent power of wisdom appeared upon His head and there came forth out of the ethers the Great White Brotherhood, the chosen sacred instruments of the Gods. Clothed in silence and power, with the fate of the world in Their hands, They moved in accord with the Cosmic Plan, so that we mortals of flesh may rise in spirit and understanding.

SPIRITUAL ART

I heard the tone of a gong singing through space.

Upon this wave, a Being of Light descends with scepter in hand, and strikes a chord within my being. The seven lights of my soul burst into flame, glowing with the fire of another universe.

As I approach my canvas with brush in hand, Cosmic Beings step out of etheric space, and visions of a more beautiful world pass before me. The light of the Cosmos streams upon my being. I move on a different plane and I breathe, enraptured, the breath of the Universal Soul.

I create a symbol that speaks unto me without voice, saying, "I am the spirit of this painting. I descend upon earth and take form upon this canvas square. I live on this canvas, not to cover a wall or to match a chair—but I am a living being. Follow me upon this vibration, on this canvas square, and I will lead you to worlds, you know not where."

A WORLD OF COLOR

Color in the astral worlds is living and sparkling substance, alive with forces. Sound and
color are the same. Every color has its own
musical note.

I move across the threshold into the astral
worlds, now, looking out from a great cliff,
across a panorama that seems to stretch a great
distance before me. The whole scene is dazzling in prismatic colors. It fills my being with
joy.

Huge swirling masses of blue pass before me
over the valley—a beautiful, vivid blue that
gives off the sound of a sombre bell, like a
gong. The blue masses come toward me and
envelop my being. Instantly a peace and love
come over me and my body rings with the
tone of the blue. I have become one with the
blue forces of love and peace. In a while they
leave me.

Then yellow-golden masses pass across the valley scene and envelop me as the blue did before. This color gave off the sound of a clear
bell, and when this color enveloped my beng,
I felt a tingling all over me. My mind became
very bright and alert, and the sound of the bell

rang through my body. These golden-yellow forces caused my mind to work with unusual clearness.

Then I beheld a very brilliant red moving before me in huge clouds. It gave off a droning sound like that of a low cymbal. This color enveloped me also, and I felt a charge of energy and power go through the body, and the sound of the cymbal rang through my being. Then this color passed on and I felt transformed.

When I returned to my body I was a new being, transmuted by the Cosmic forces of light, sound, and color.

FULL MOON MEDITATION

This moment is full of promise, for a psychic door is open when the moon is full.

A TEMPLE IN THE HIMALAYAS

I turned my eyes toward the Temple of Wisdom. I concentrated my mind upon the focal point of light and I saw a Temple in the vast region of Tibet, resting upon a rock for untold centuries.

Here the Sages of Wisdom drank the divine nectar as it poured in a stream from the higher worlds. The Masters of Wisdom instructed humanity with an unseen hand and directed the affairs of the multitude.

This Temple upon a rock, blazing with the purity of Cosmic light, is acting as a gyroscope for the world. This Temple of Wisdom on a rock is unseen and unknown to humanity, yet all is known to Them, the Masters of Wisdom, for Their rays descend upon all.

I AM AN OPEN BOOK

Do you ask me for recommendations? Read the symbols upon my face. They are the keys to the sacred inner chambers. Look at my eyes and see the soul. The sound of my voice is the tone of my being. Look at my hands and watch my stride. Can't you recognize the signs? There is nothing hidden. Everything you want to know is shown to you by a sign.

I HEAR THE VOICES OF CHILDREN

I hear the voices of children
upon the green,
a group of children singing, singing
as they danced upon the green.
A children's song, a mystic song,
sung by children on the green.
As if a host of angels sang,
through the children rang the song
as they danced upon the green.

A child's song, yet a universal song,
sung by children on the green.
A host of angels sang
through the children's song,
and through the children's song
the host of angels sing a universal song
as they danced upon the green.

THE SPIRIT OF NATURE

The earth and sky merge with the river and
mountain. A spirit moves through the forest.
Nature becomes an open book.

I BECAME A WHITE FLOWER

I became as a white flower in meadows that slept. The mountains were still, the sky was speechless. In this stillness I was taught of activity beyond mortal sight.

MYSTIC ART

I step aside from the whirl and strain of city streets into my studio silence. There I dwell until a phosphorescent cloud of love around me glows.

And through the garden of my soul I roam, and I heard it spoken unto me without voice, "Art is that substance before the world was. It is life, love, and creation." I walked into the Temple of Ancient Wisdom and dipped my brush into the Cosmic pool of soul which reflects the worlds beyond time and space.

THE SHADED PATH

I doubted the forces that govern my destiny. I was torn with the emotions and the conflict of a double mind. So I turned on the Dark Path to the left.

This lower vibration felt like cold, clammy hands creeping over me. The door within my heart closed to the higher worlds. The flame of faith was no more in my heart. My body became dark like a tomb and I lived in the miserable land of materialism—dead, in the land of the living dead, bodies moving without a single breath of spirit, robots and tools for some dark force, and walking the path of futility and illusion.

THE KEY TO KNOWING

I inquired and the answer came.

I asked of man. He gave me little. I searched in ancient writings and they gave me only a key. With it I opened the door to the vast and great unknown. Here I spoke and an answer came. Here I searched and I found the jewel. I inquired of all things, and all things came unto me. No barrier, no time, no space—I became one with all, and all things lived within me.

A NEW BIRTH

I met my counterpart, who had descended from the other world to meet me upon this material plane. Love streamed through me like a river of light. Her being fired my soul to unlimited heights.

In silent love we dwelt, and it grew like a ball of fire around us. Out of this fire I heard a ring like the tone of the spheres. Upon this rhythm a blue light descended into the fire. It spun and grew, and lo, we beheld a form divine, a radiant and happy child born of pure love and light. The child stepped forth from the fire upon our threshold, clothed with body to dwell with us upon our earth plane.

TO A FRIEND

My heart glows like the full-orbed setting sun, fanned by the sacred breath of my love for a friend who can merge with me. What greater gift can man possess than a friend vibrating with the rhythm of your own being? It is enough for me to know a person like thee, for it fires my being to unlimited heights and gives me power to walk upon my path.

I GO TO A TEACHER

They say that he is a Master. I hope he is. For some time I searched for one.

I look forward for days to our meeting, and as the hour approaches, with reverence do I enter his abode. As I shake his hand I search his face with burning eyes and go over his features, looking for a sign of his true being. Of a sudden, something happens within my solar plexus, for there is no response to my burning search.

I seem to be alone. I become weary and heavy and I want to get away, for this person is not my teacher.

DEATH UPON THE SEA

We sailed upon the sea on a gray and quiet day. Out of nowhere a great wind blew up, and before long a black hurricane was upon us.

The howling wind and lashing waves tore relentlessly at the ship. Wild cries—wet clothes— the shrieking wind blinded us. Our only thought was a place on solid land. But it was no use—the ship was sinking and each one was dazed with his own desire for rescue. We sank beneath the cold waters, gasping for air. And then darkness came upon me and consciousness was no more.

When I recovered my sense of awareness I was standing upon floating wreckage, watching the dead bodies as they bobbed upon the sea. A strong light piercing the clouds—the storm was over, and a gentle breeze blew upon the waters.

I thought of the calm sea and I found myself walking upon the water, to my surprise. A strange feeling came over me, because I did not sink beneath the cold black waters. I stooped to pick up a board floating on the water, and to my surprise, my hand passed through the board as if it were air. Now I know this is not my material body. I almost screamed as I looked about me and suddenly saw before me, my body, dead upon the angry waters.

INVISIBLE TWILIGHT HOST

Twilight Goddess,
what precious fire have You given my spirit?
Your fragrant presence,
with a host of a thousand thousand spirit forms
breaks into a divine rapture above me.

With gentle caress You sweep by
and tell me things that never die.

VISION CAME UPON ME

It was on a hill, on a warm and windy day.

I am grateful for life and grateful for the opening of the center of my being, grateful for a little understanding, and for a sense of freedom from materialism, from the race thought, and from the body.

As I bathe in the sea of Cosmic substance I wonder what is important to man. I see my answer. It is only that which elevates his soul—action outside of vanity and motives of pure love.

What can be compared to a spiritual state of being? As I gaze about me, everything seems so impersonal. It is all beyond strife, emotions, and longings—a perfect state of harmony beyond discordant mortality. What a vision of non-attachment! It breaks my earth slumber. For a moment I am separated from this earth plane. The mountain is so far away, yet all is so close to me. They speak to me in another tongue, without voice.

I am back on my hill again. From a moment of eternity, I return to my relative state on this earth plane.

ON THE THRESHOLD

I stand on the threshold of the unseen.
I see before me a shoreless sea of light.
I see beyond the pale star
an order of beauty.
I embrace the whole structure.
I am here,
I am there.

THE SPIRIT OF A VIOLIN

The spirit of a violin called to me to enter its domain. Through its radiation I entered a hall filled with a thousand spirit forms.

Swiftly and softly we winged around and through the violin domain. Down the strings, around the bridge, and through the great dome of blue we flew. These inhabitants were a happy lot who sang and danced. They told me I would see a performance.

Electrical radiations filled the dome as the master of music picked up the violin and was about to play. All became very still.

Light filled the dome as the master touched the strings. Then I heard a heavenly sound within as I never heard it without. As the master played, great throngs of spirit forms rushed through the hall like a great wind, and disappeared out into space.

I ROSE FROM THE EARTH

I rose from the earth into the blue etheric spaces, and there I hung suspended on some unseen platform, enraptured with the breathless beauty of the pristine stellar spaces.

I look toward the earth, and there I beheld the deep, rich, and luminous sphere against the darkness of the vast unknown. A sound, like some huge melodious gong, vibrated from the planets toward the earth, and the stars sang a melody in their path through the universe.

I turn toward the earth and see the North Pole smile with a sparkling white toward the sun. I cannot believe there are millions upon millions of human beings down there.

How different the world becomes when I am detached. It is surely the beginning of great wisdom.

INITIATION

Initiation into the mysteries of Nature is the union of the mind and heart with the forces of the Cosmos. The union of the soul with the Universal Soul causes the body to weaken its hold upon the mind. The mind is free to explore realms beyond time and space.

The gate of the heart is opened. The seven mystic eyes of the body are opened to the sacred truths that are closed to the mortal eye. Man's vision becomes keen and broad. He becomes detached from the small circles of intolerance and self and merges with the infinite circle of the Cosmic Intelligence. His body is not a vehicle for pleasure and selfish actions, but is a sacred instrument for the great forces of the universe that work for the good of humanity.

THE VALLEY OF SHADOWS

I took the narrow path that would lead me to the Temple of Wisdom, when suddenly I found myself in the Valley of Shadows, full of hideous shapes and forms. I saw the Temple in the distance far beyond this region. I continued walking through this place of ugly forms who watched my steps and read my thoughts. They rolled clouds of fear against me to weaken my will. But they did not affect me, and I continued through this place unafraid.

The secret of these shadowy creatures is to cause fear in a person's heart. And if accepted, the fear would give the shadowy forms the power of life to move against me. But I moved through the shadows without fear because I felt the faith of the spiritual forces within.

INTRUSION

There was a rush of thought through my study, phosphorescent, yet not seen, like a strong current rushing on through my study.

"Who is it?" I called. "And where are you from?" But there was no answer to where it came from and where it went. A strange unfamiliar being on its way to a strange and unknown place.

THE BLUE CHAMBER OF THE HEART

In a quiet place I enter the silent region of the mind, and there I still the voices of the body. In this silence I enter a greater silence of the heart.

Here I am free from the body and the clamor of the world. I listen to the inflow of intuition. The knowledge beyond time and space sweeps into my heart, gently telling me many things the mind did not know. I enter the blue chamber of the heart and see before me a dazzling world of color and beauty.

With courage and will I walked the chamber of blue into the luminous world of beauty and harmony far beyond our world of form.

A RARE FLOWER

Among deserted factories and building places
I have my dwelling place.

A rain of thought fell upon my barren place
and watered the whole ground.
Thoughts of beauty and love
brought forth a rare flower
upon my barren floor.

I fled to the wild wood
and the rugged blue mountain
and lived upon the scented pine air.
But nowhere in all Nature
could I a flower find
like the delicate creature that grew
upon my barren floor.

THE TEMPLE OF SPIRIT

A group of Adepts in a temple put their bodies in a deep trance. They rose in spirit to another world and there they met in a Temple of spirit. In this Temple built without hands they put their astral bodies in a deep trance and rose in spirit to the celestial world, and they met in a Temple made of Cosmic light. To this Temple the Lords of the World came and taught them many things never whispered by any mortal man. The Adepts received the keys to immortality and the rod of power with which they controlled all forces on the earth.

PILAR HILL

On a hill beside the canyon, I lived and com-
muned with Nature. The mountains and the
sky lived within me.

THE HERMETIC MARRIAGE

Man's illumination and complete union with the Universal Forces are depicted in the drama of the heavens through the marriage of the Sun and the Moon. The positive, male element of the Sun, or brain, and the negative, female element of the Moon, or the heart are used as symbols in the secret doctrine to hide the true meaning from the world.

This key unlocks the inner chambers of man's being, where one finds the portal to the higher worlds. The key is fashioned out of the substance of love, will, and courage, and is able to unlock the immortal gates that lead to the worlds hung suspended in the Heart of the Cosmos.

BECAUSE I AM UNIVERSAL

I am as a roaring lion at noonday.
I am as silent as night.
I am the ocean and the sky,
I am the mountains and the rivers.
I am the woman loving her child.
I am the derelict and tramp.
I am the Christ worshipped by the multitudes.
I am everywhere because I am universal.
And with this body, upon this earth plane
I pass.

THE OFFERING

As an offering I cast my soul before the feet
of a friend as a cloak before the muddy pools.
But he stamped and wiped his feet upon my
spotless offering, and left me stained and
broken.

THE ALTAR FLAME

O burning flame of quiet light,
glowing, glowing in my soul tonight,
has my spirit taken form within thy Cosmic
flame?

O radiant beauty, glow, delight,
glowing with life all through the night,
burning, burning on the boundless shore of
beauty,
bright mystic flame of ancient lore,
rising in my heart like a brazen serpent,
steady burning, turning in my soul
till a magic cloth is spun of gems
of light and fire,
to robe me in diadems
of universal attire.

Your soundless voice speaks the language of
my soul,
O spark of divinity,
eternal sentinel of the dark abode.
In still stillness your fire within my body
glows,
as if upon the altar my soul lies burning,
burning to the Avatar.
With hypnotic stare and mysterious glow,
my spirit thou hast captured from this body
of woe.

Prostrate I remain before thy light
while my soul glows in painful delight
on the altar in nightmares of human strife.
Thus, thus I am born to newer life.

THE HEALING

My body groans with pain and my mind is tormented with a thousand demons. All my strength is gone and I have not the will to endure this suffering. I reach out toward space and the depths of my soul cry out to the Beings That walk upon the pristine stellar spaces.

In a moment I feel as if some electrical current breaks and my aura is flooded with a beautiful blue, intense and sparkling. Peace and harmony pour upon me like the soft glow of a sunbeam at dawn. I draw a long breath, as if to drink yet deeper this divine outpouring.

My call was answered and I beheld a spirit at my side, like some God, whose grace and power gave me food for many days.

A DIVINE PRESENCE

We are now ushered into God's presence. This room is no longer a barrier to the higher worlds. The walls are dissolved, the furniture disappears. The Cosmic winds sweep through, and out of a mist, a beautiful vista takes shape. A flash of Cosmic power burst into this sacred abode and a dazzling electrical substance filled the whole room. I breathe enraptured this vibrating presence of liquid light which transforms my body into a Temple of Cosmic Fire.

The presence of God has become my breath, my blood, and my body. I live as long as this presence is with me, and every moment I feel the breath of the Cosmic Presence.

A SHADOW UPON THE RIVER

While I cross the River of Truth to my Temple on the other shore, a gigantic spectre created by fear and doubt hung by the Temple site.

THE MAGICIAN

I drew a circle around me, and in the center I made a star. I placed the four elements on the north, west, east, and south sides of the circle, and in the center I stood with my magic rod. And I called forth the spirits of the air, who answered my call and became the instruments of my will.

COSMIC ART

Cosmic Art is spirit—it is the language of the Gods. It is the Pathway to the mystery of life and death. Cosmic Art is the breath of the world, it is the beginning and the end, it is the gate to the higher worlds. Cosmic Art is the key to man, it is the key to Nature, it is the key to things visible and invisible.

Cosmic Art leads to the supreme moment in life, an experience we bring out of the vast unknown—when we blend our being with the Cosmos and identify ourselves as we walk the Road of Life across this material planet. Cosmic Art brings the heart, mind, and body under the rays of the Cosmic forces, giving the experience of pure joy, of spiritual light, and universal life, a life that is beyond time or space.

THE FLIGHT IN SPACE

With a terrific spiral motion I left the earth for another land. I shot through the ether and then hung suspended on some platform unseen. I heard chords of music and saw wide passes of color across space—gold, green, and red, down to the thundering purple below me. And I heard the melody like that of a harp above me. It uncovered the gate to another world. I passed through like some gentle wind.

A GLOW WITHIN

I seem to walk in a dark valley. I would die before I reached the mountain if it were not for a glow within my being.

My intense desire for knowledge and creative art changes my humble dwelling into a garden of paradise, and my bread and tea become a feast for the Gods. Every move I make, I know the divine powers of destiny are working through me.

MY BELOVED

Lords of Flame, Great White Brotherhood,
through Thy sacred breath,
from a mortal of flesh I become immortal.
Through Thy holy touch,
from a grain of sand I become a star.

My God, my Beloved, all things of the earth
have become as dust, and there is nothing here
for me. Only in Your embrace do I live and
breathe. All else is death and decay and glitter
but for a moment.

My only desire is to become one with Thy
sacred Being, for when Thy holy Love descends upon me, I become as great as the universe and the great vault of the heavens is
within me. And as I stand on the brink of eternity, in the deep purple of Thy consciousness, I
can see You face to face.

Out of the mystery of the heavens beyond the
heavens, Your divine Being has come forth
fashioned in Cosmic Fire. Your intense purity
blesses the whole universe. Out of Your eyes
issue floods of magnetic light that descend like
a healing wave. Your voice is like soft music,
yet it is also so great that it thunders through
the blackness of the outer universe.

My Beloved, who can measure Your wisdom, or describe the wonders of Your Being? For there is nothing in this world that can be compared to Thee.

O Lord, I ask for nothing in this world or any other world but for Thy countenance to shine down upon me, for it is only then that I begin to live. Let my personality dissolve. And may Thy cloak come upon me, O Holy One. May all my desire perish, so that Thy Light will burn clearly within my being.

I live with but one hope in my heart, and that is to become one with Thy Being. Without Thee, I am lower than the worm. But through Thy sacred touch I become Thy Son. And as a Son of God all things are mine, for Thou hast given all to Thy Son.

Blessed be the name of the Lord of Light, the Holy of Holies, the beginning and the end, now and forever.

INDEX BY TITLE

INDEX BY SUBJECT

EXPERIENCES IN THIS WORLD

Communion with Daily Life

TRIALS ON THE PATH

SPIRITUAL FRIENDSHIP

148